The Journey of Baby Angel...

By

TRACI WATERS, GRAMMIE

COPYRIGHT

Copyright @ 2021 by
Traci Waters

ALL RIGHTS RESERVED. NO part of this book may be reproduced or transmitted in any form by any means, electronic or mechanical, including photocopying and recording, or by any information storage and retrieval system, except as may be expressly permitted in writing from the author.

ISBN: 978-1-0880-2397-6

Printed in the United States of America

This book is dedicated to *Grammie's Love, Rory Daniella.*

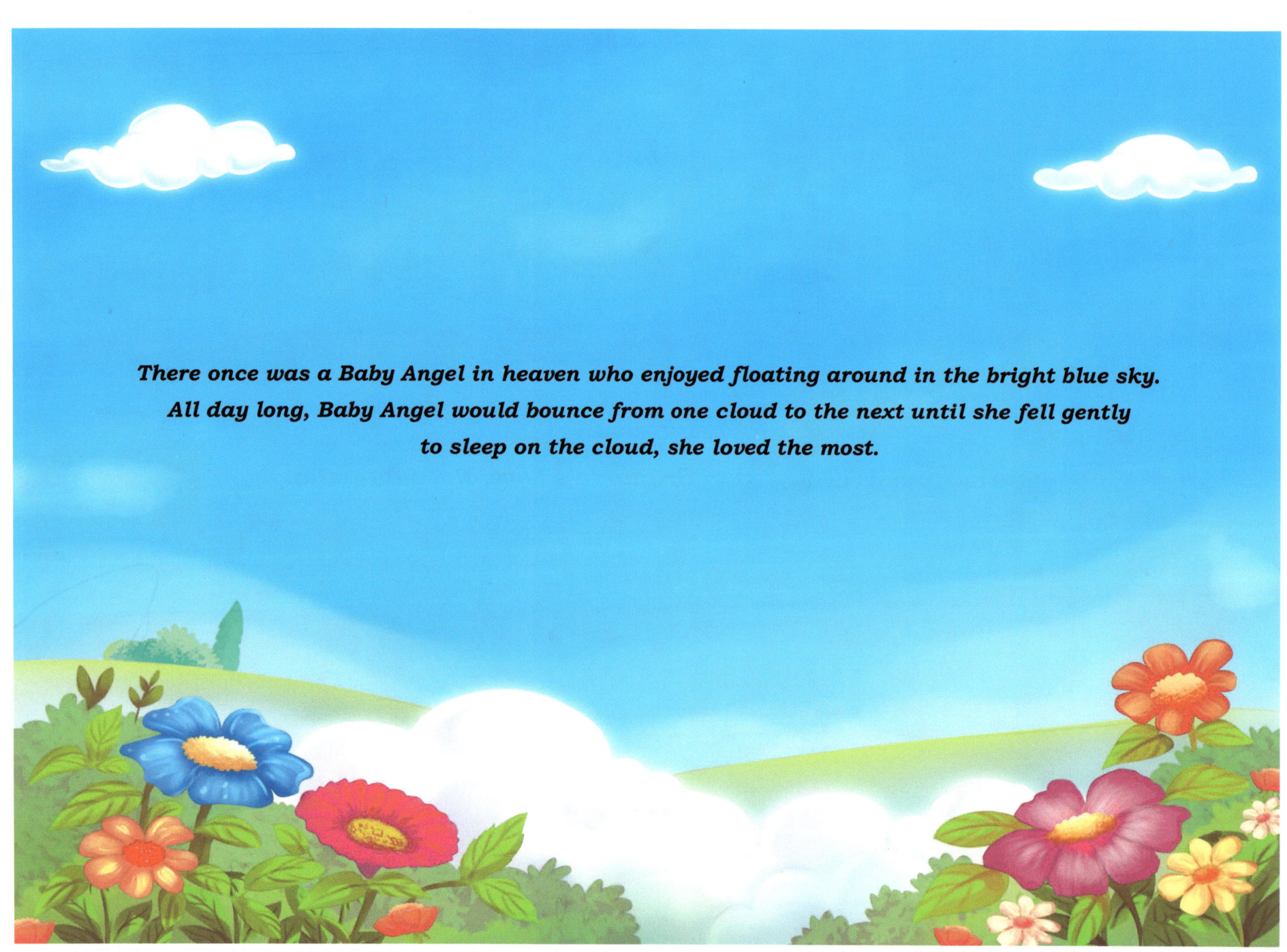

There once was a Baby Angel in heaven who enjoyed floating around in the bright blue sky. All day long, Baby Angel would bounce from one cloud to the next until she fell gently to sleep on the cloud, she loved the most.

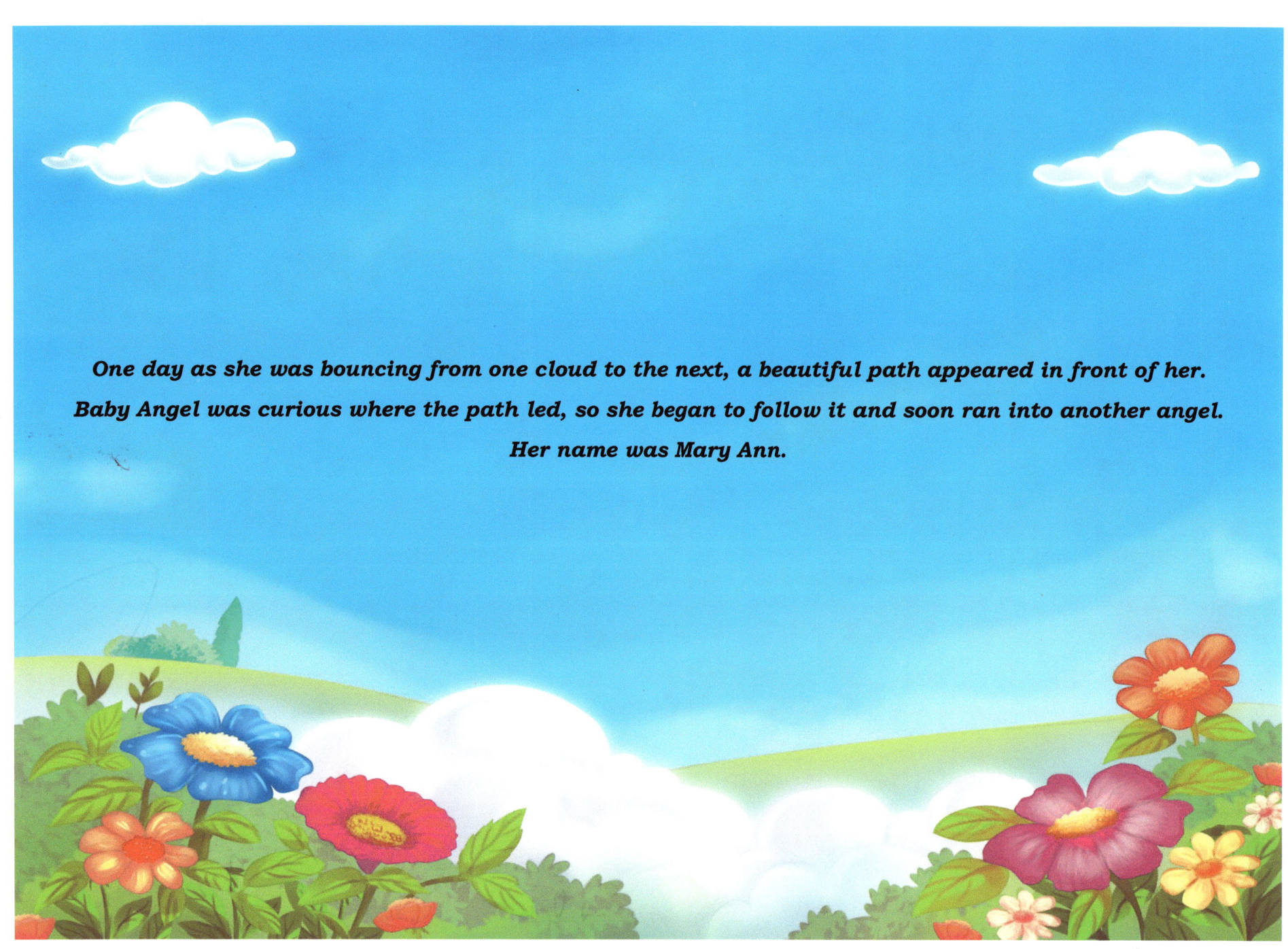

One day as she was bouncing from one cloud to the next, a beautiful path appeared in front of her. Baby Angel was curious where the path led, so she began to follow it and soon ran into another angel. Her name was Mary Ann.

"How are you Baby Angel," Mary Ann asked.

"I am just fine, thank you very much. This path appeared and I am curious where it leads" Baby Angel replied.

"This is the start of your journey, you will find beautiful things along the way," Mary Ann replied.

"Stay on the path and you will end up just where you belong sweet girl."

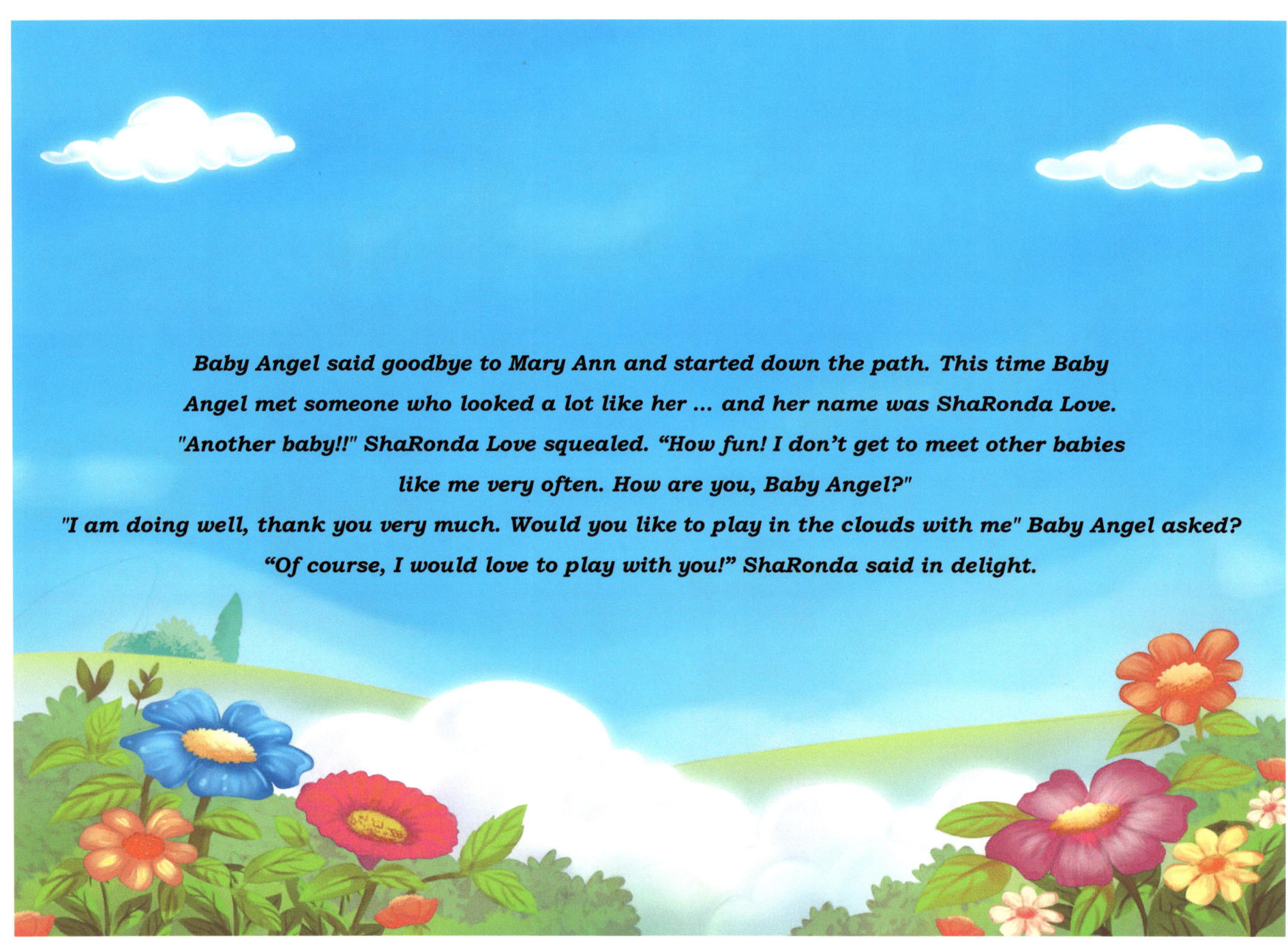

Baby Angel said goodbye to Mary Ann and started down the path. This time Baby Angel met someone who looked a lot like her ... and her name was ShaRonda Love.
"Another baby!!" ShaRonda Love squealed. "How fun! I don't get to meet other babies like me very often. How are you, Baby Angel?"
"I am doing well, thank you very much. Would you like to play in the clouds with me" Baby Angel asked?
"Of course, I would love to play with you!" ShaRonda said in delight.

The two babies played and played and played in the fluffy white clouds until the path appeared again.

"I see the path ShaRonda, it must be time for me to leave" Baby Angel said.

"I enjoyed playing with you, Baby Angel. I am going to tell my mama all about our day!"

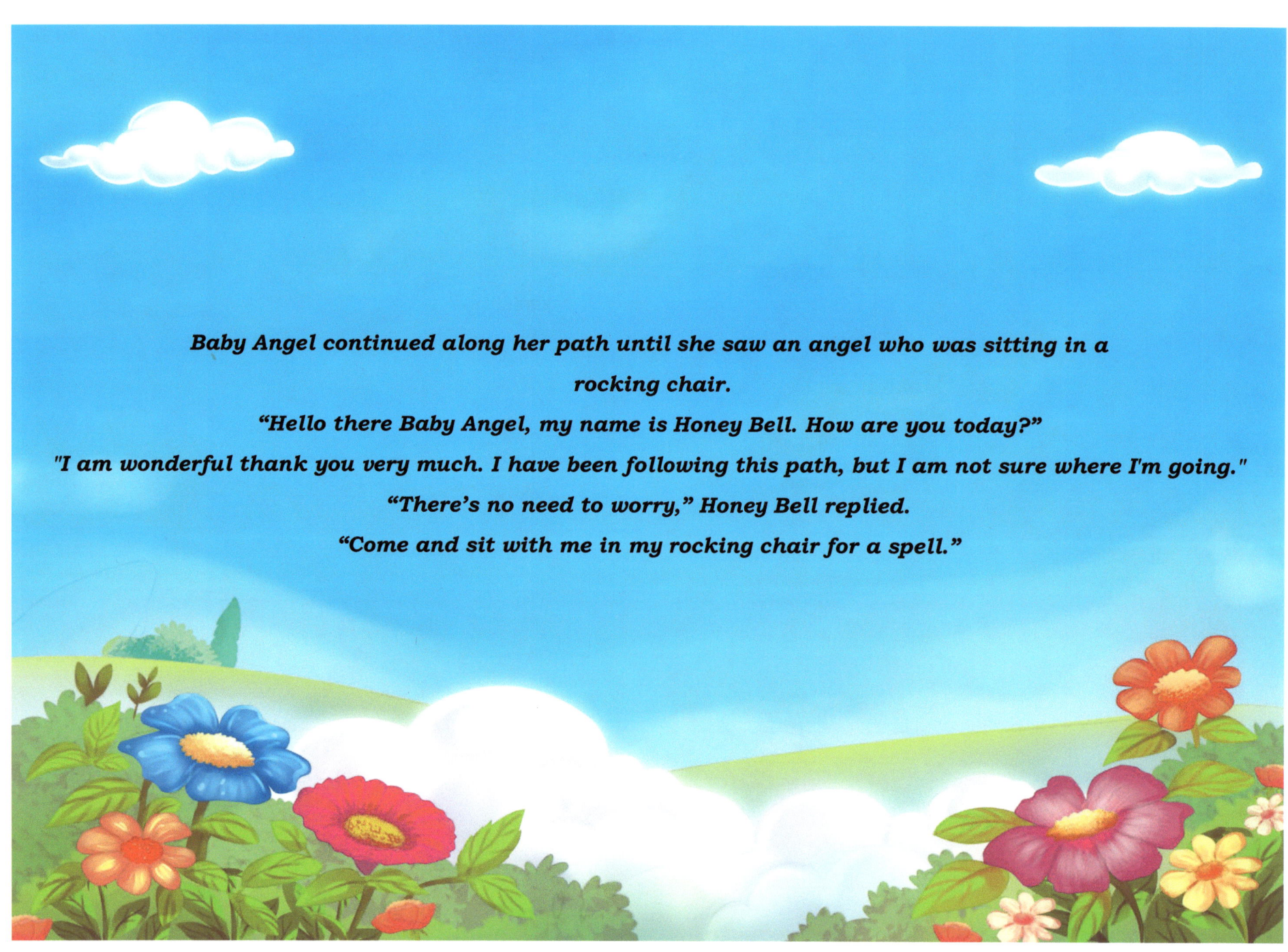

Baby Angel continued along her path until she saw an angel who was sitting in a rocking chair.

"Hello there Baby Angel, my name is Honey Bell. How are you today?"

"I am wonderful thank you very much. I have been following this path, but I am not sure where I'm going."

"There's no need to worry," Honey Bell replied.

"Come and sit with me in my rocking chair for a spell."

Honey Bell sat Baby Angel on her lap, and they rocked and rocked and rocked in that old chair. Baby Angel began to feel comforted and at ease. After spending some time together, Honey Bell told her, "It's time for you to continue along your path little one."

As she continued, Baby Angel came across a beautiful pond and yet another angel.

She said "Hey there Baby Angel, my name is Mae Ella. How are you today?"

"I am excellent thank you very much. What are you doing" Baby Angel asked?

"I am trying to catch a fish. Do you know how to fish," Mae Ella asked?

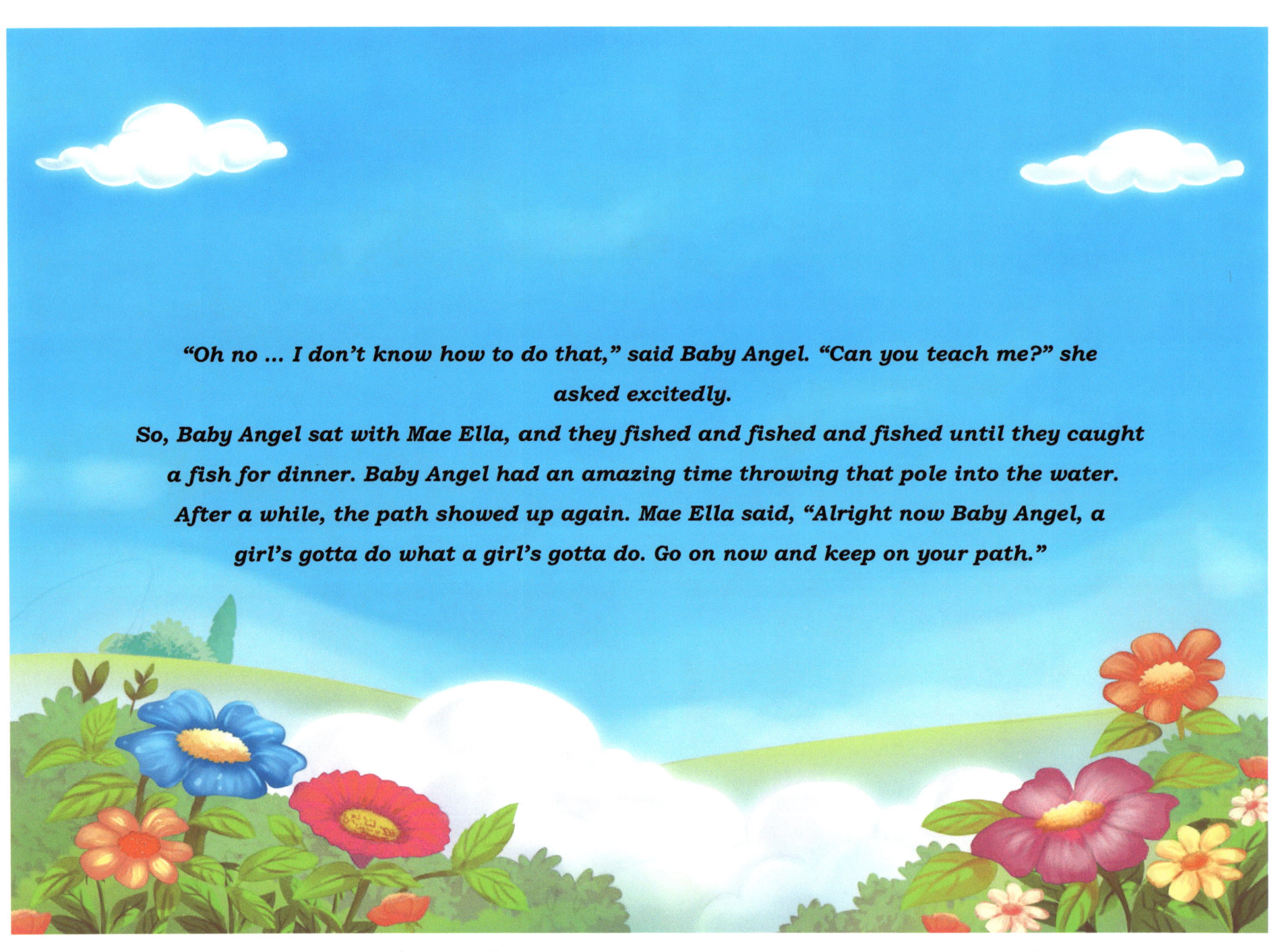

"Oh no ... I don't know how to do that," said Baby Angel. "Can you teach me?" she asked excitedly.

So, Baby Angel sat with Mae Ella, and they fished and fished and fished until they caught a fish for dinner. Baby Angel had an amazing time throwing that pole into the water. After a while, the path showed up again. Mae Ella said, "Alright now Baby Angel, a girl's gotta do what a girl's gotta do. Go on now and keep on your path."

Baby Angel continued down the path, anxious to see what she would find next.
This time she saw two angels sitting on the front porch of their house telling stories and laughing!
One of the angels was really, really funny. Her name was Delma, but she said everyone called her Netta.
The other angel said her name was Mary, but everyone called her Nei Nei.

Baby Angel listened to Netta tell her stories, and she laughed and laughed and laughed. Netta was the funniest angel she had ever met.

After the last story was told, Baby Angel noticed that the path had appeared again. She told them that she wanted to stay and hear more of Netta's stories, but Nei Nei picked her up and they started down the path together.

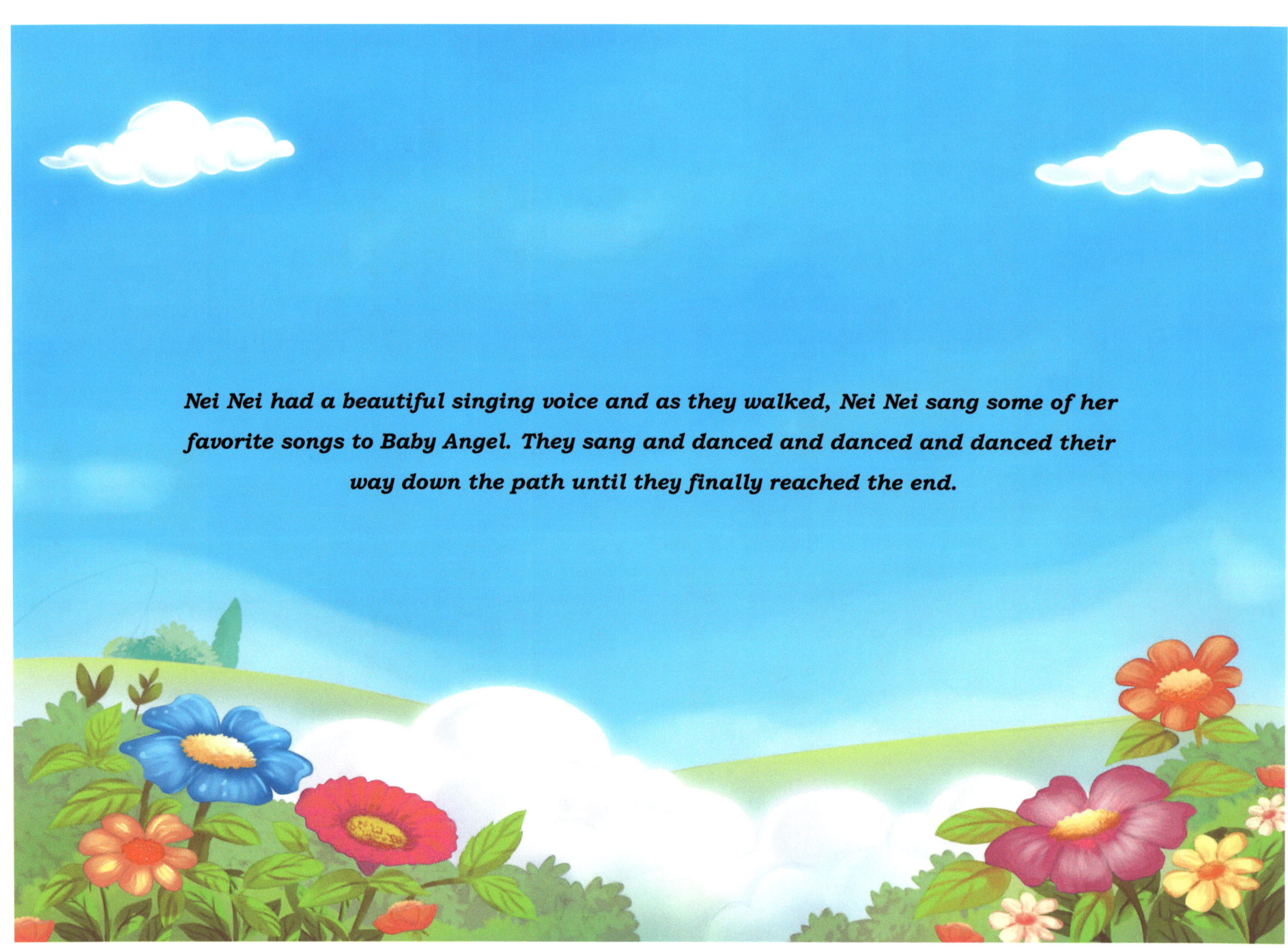

Nei Nei had a beautiful singing voice and as they walked, Nei Nei sang some of her favorite songs to Baby Angel. They sang and danced and danced and danced their way down the path until they finally reached the end.

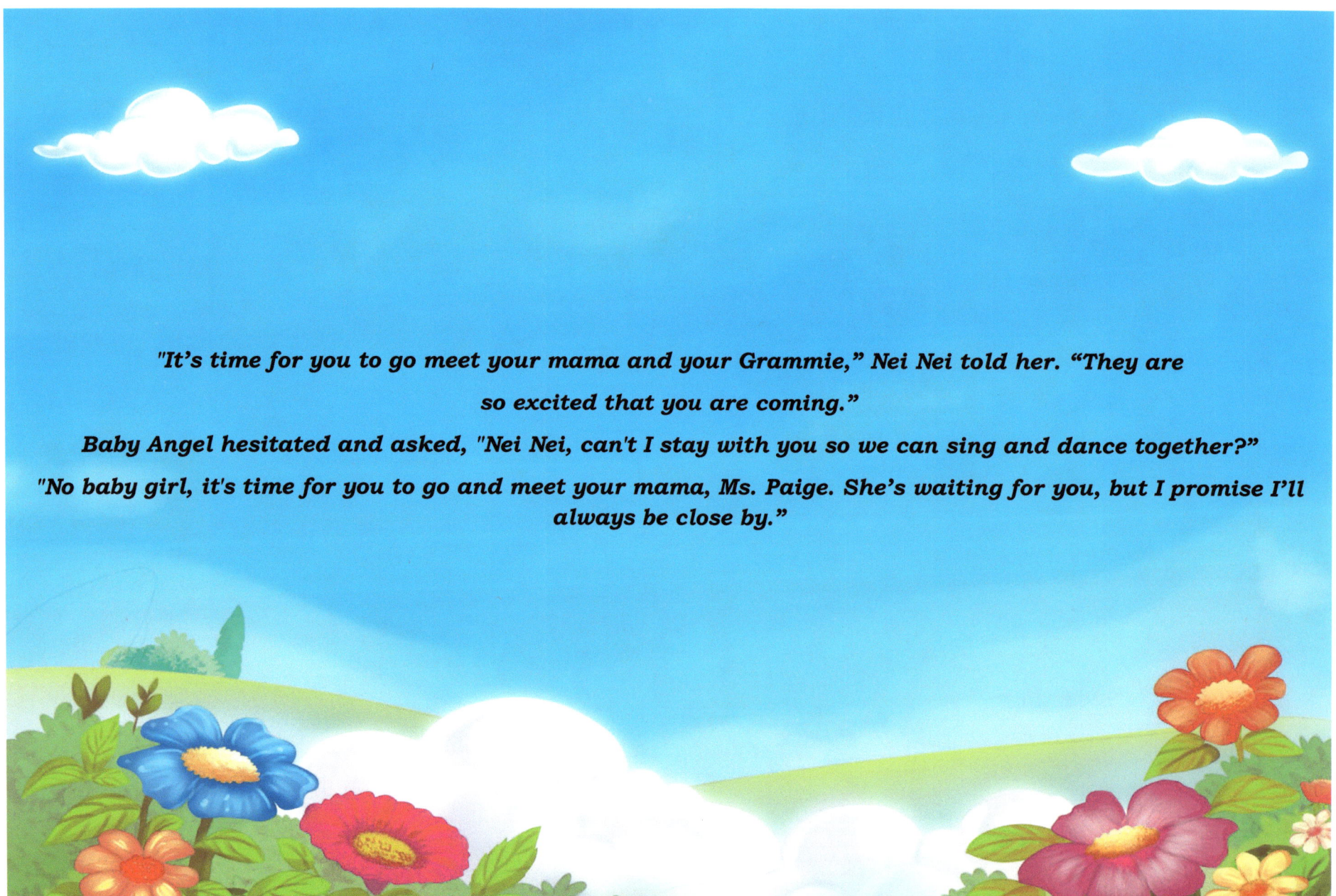

"It's time for you to go meet your mama and your Grammie," Nei Nei told her. "They are so excited that you are coming."

Baby Angel hesitated and asked, "Nei Nei, can't I stay with you so we can sing and dance together?"

"No baby girl, it's time for you to go and meet your mama, Ms. Paige. She's waiting for you, but I promise I'll always be close by."

Nei Nei kissed Baby Angel on the cheek and told her she loved her.

Then suddenly, Baby Angel took an enormous bounce.

She bounced and bounced and bounced.

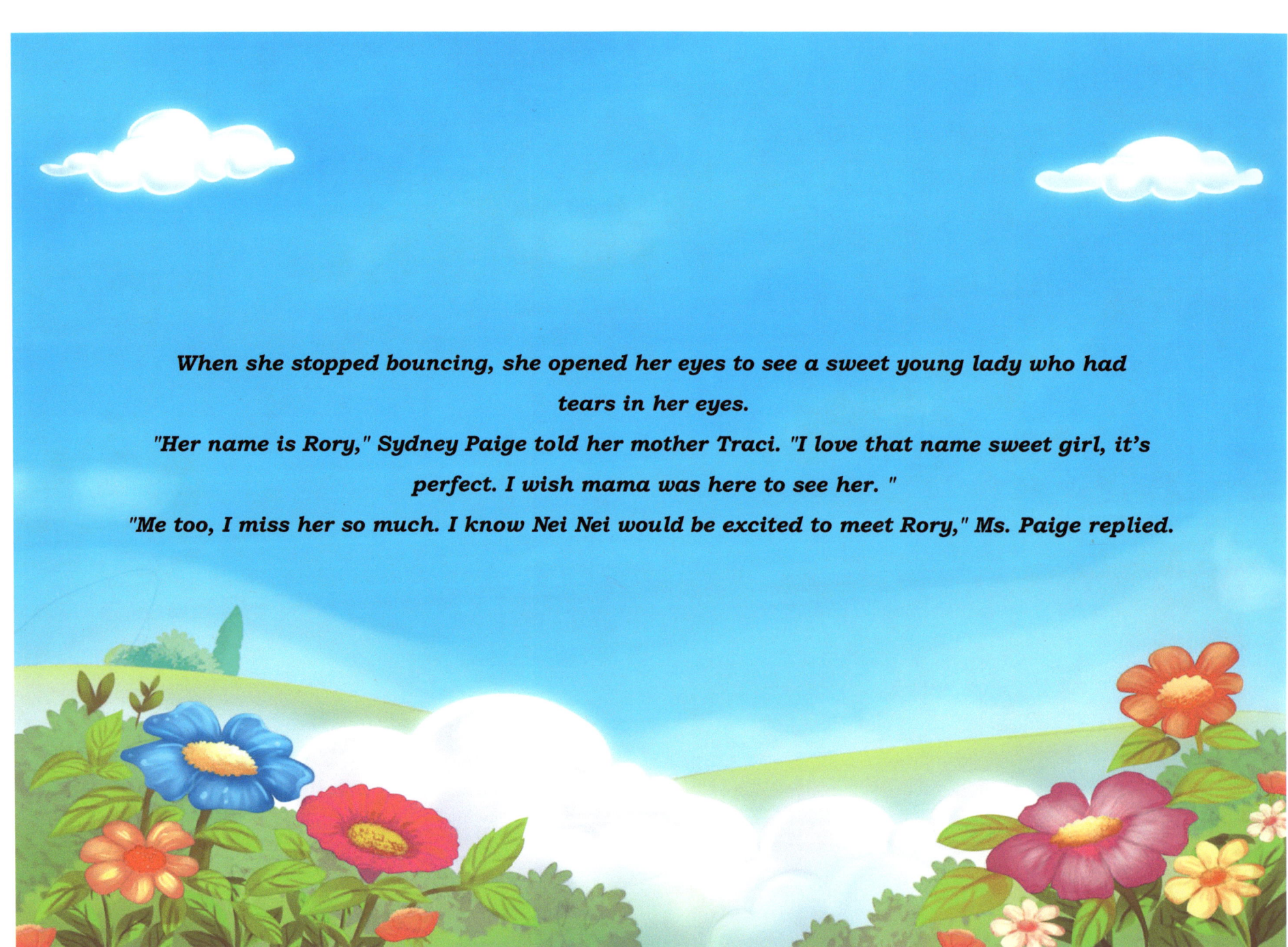

When she stopped bouncing, she opened her eyes to see a sweet young lady who had tears in her eyes.

"Her name is Rory," Sydney Paige told her mother Traci. "I love that name sweet girl, it's perfect. I wish mama was here to see her."

"Me too, I miss her so much. I know Nei Nei would be excited to meet Rory," Ms. Paige replied.

As she grew, Grammie taught Rory all about her family tree.
Her Great, great, great grandmothers, Mary Ann and Honey Bell,
her Great, Great Grandmother, Mae Ella,
her Great, Great Auntie, Netta,
her Great Auntie ShaRonda,
and her Great Grandmother Nei, Nei.

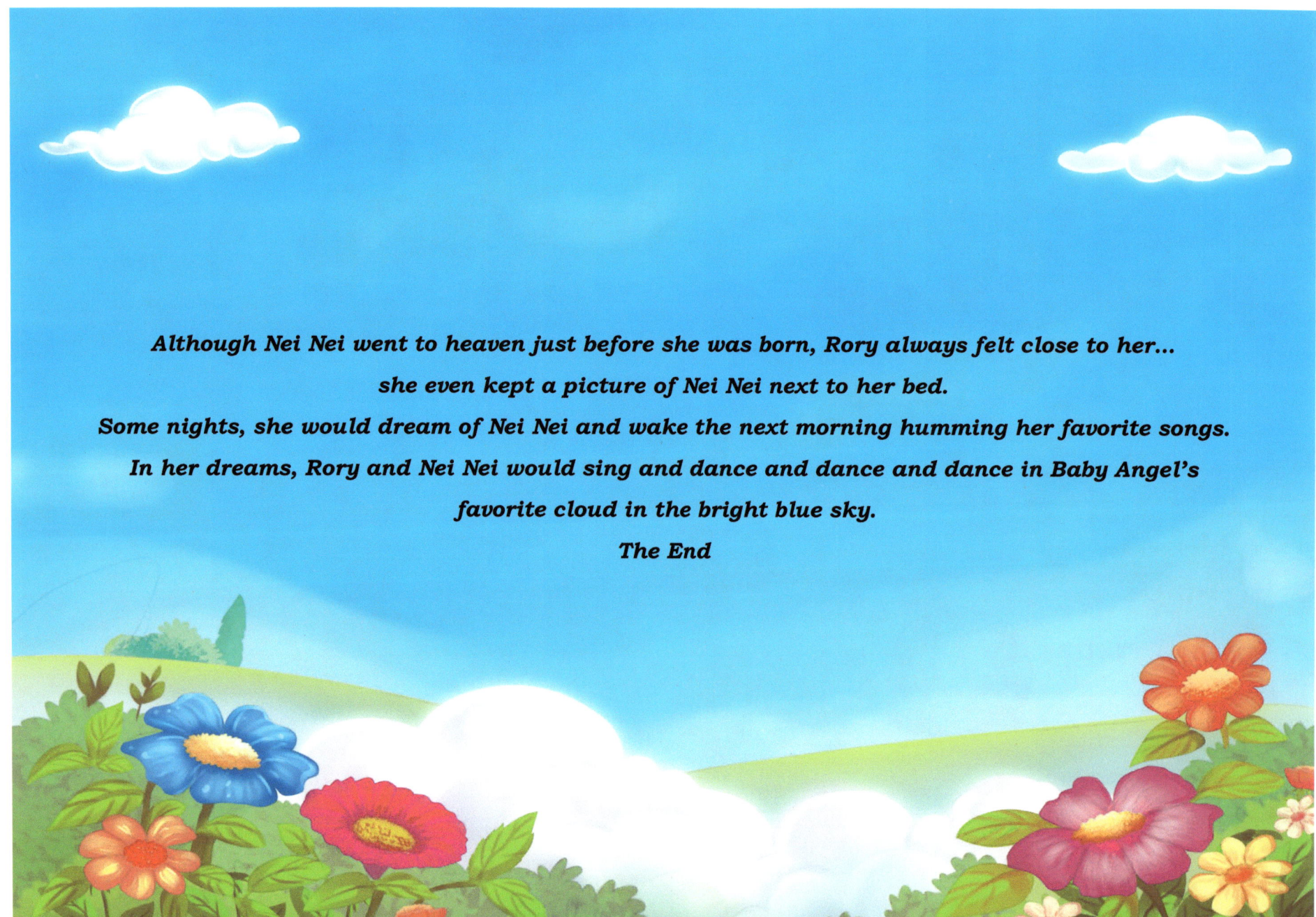

*Although Nei Nei went to heaven just before she was born, Rory always felt close to her...
she even kept a picture of Nei Nei next to her bed.
Some nights, she would dream of Nei Nei and wake the next morning humming her favorite songs.
In her dreams, Rory and Nei Nei would sing and dance and dance and dance in Baby Angel's
favorite cloud in the bright blue sky.*

The End

HOPKINSVILLE-CHRISTIAN CO PUBLIC LIBRARY

3 KSPE 004 06111 H

CPSIA information can be obtained
at www.ICGtesting.com
Printed in the USA
LVHW011702060522
717886LV00003B/30